YOUR ONE AND ONLY

TRAVEL GUIDE TO PAPUA, WEST PAPUA & PAPUA NEW GUINEA

110% freshly researched in 2023 by
Chief Red Feather and Craig Antweiler

INTRO

This guide is completely biased, has neither been verified, layouted or reviewed and the authors are two weirds (white, educated, industrialized, rich, democratic) that just happened to venture to mystic and dangerous Papua much to their families horror. That's why we wanted the guide book to be as affordable as your favorite juicy sweet potato Kumpir around the corner.

Sit back and enjoy the following mess - it will prepare you for an adventurous journey to Papua - the home of crazy. We'll cover everything from itineraries to the last chapter „Hygiene" where we include a couple of empty pages that you can use as toilet paper in Papua when needed.

3

MANAGEMENT SUMMARY

Papua is intense, not safe and very friendly.

To get an idea of the colorful, warm hearted Papuans check out @dawnofdurian Instagram Papua highlight.

Your best resource is this guide book and inviting the authors to a dinner with you including transport and accommodation.

With visa on arrival for many tourists to Indonesia you really just need a valid previledged passport and find a flight to Jakarta, Manado or Makassar to transfer to a domestic flight to Papua.

For PNG many visitors will get a visa on arrival for free only at Port Moresby airport on flights from pacific neighboring countries.

PAPUA TRAVEL GUIDE

Itineraries

Hiking in the Baliem Valley

UNDERSTAND

Papua is actually two parts: West Papua (former Irian Jaya) of Indonesia in the West and ther rest that comprises the Papua New Guinea sovereign country that you have never heard of before. In this book we don't use the geographic names consistently as is common in Papua. Here's a self drawn map:

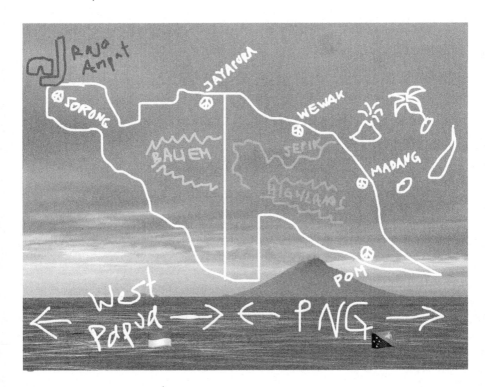

PAPUA VISA(S)

As of 2023 citizens of many countries like the European Union can get a visa on arrival for 35$ and 30 days at the Indonesian entry airports and for free for 90 days at the PNG entry airports. Both are single entry visas.

It is valid until you get robbed. But then there are other challenges (compare chapter on repatriating coffins and how to avoid holdups).

If you plan to re-enter Indonesia through the only land border at Wutung near Jayapura plan to have your visa valid and ready. There is an Indonesian consulate in Vanimo 1h from the border.

Pro tip: Don't loose your passport. One the plus side you'll notice early since it'll be checked multiple times a day ;-)

ARRIVAL AT DOMINE EDUARD OSOK INTERNATIONAL AIRPORT

Sorong has no international flights though. It's quite modern and has a few ATMs that accept international credit cards. Mandiri seams to work best.

As in many countries, once you leave the terminal building some taxi drivers might approach you. But it's way less offensive that let's say Bali or in India.

The airport is east of the city center within walking distance from the ferry terminal.

The cheapest option is getting a minibus form just outside the the airport premises on the main road. They take you for 5k IDR each to the city center or ferry terminal.

11

Depending on the time of arrival you can get a SIM card and exchange money at the airport. If the shops are closed you'll surely find someone who can exchange you some small amount and share their internet hotspot for some time. The locals are so helpful all the time and most will either speak some English or can call someone to translate for them.

SIM-CARD

There are three main mobile providers in West Papua.

- Telkomsel (best for West Papua)
- Three and
- Other providers.

When buying a SIM card you'll most likely be registered on a visitors SIM card that expires after a month. You can charge the SIM card virtually in all towns and villages with scratch cards. 20GB cost around 150k IDR including the SIM card.

In PNG just use the cheap SIM test kit allowances with all three providers.

15

MONEY

US dollars: April 2023: 1 USD = 15.100 IDR).

Euro: April 2023: 1 EUR = 16.700 IDR

A rule of thumb is that one million Indonesian rupiah is 60€.

You can exchange US Dollars almost anywhere for even better rates than your bank offers o.O Even private vendors or your friends might offer to exchange. Euros are accepted for a somewhat worse but still acceptable rates.

An increasing number of ATMs offer Visa / MasterCard credit card withdrawals. But don't rely too much on them. Especially away from the large cities. Look out for Bank Mandiri ATMs for example.

16

SECURITY

Obviously Papua is not as safe as Iraq. Quite the opposite: PNG is known for really bad security ranging from frequent street holdups by the notorious Raskols to kidnappings for ransom.

For psychological protection Try to steal a shield from Port Moresby's great national museum:

Almost all cities of PNG are no-go-areas. Especially the Capital Port Moresby often listed most dangerous city around the world. (West Papua is safe though). Be alert and ask locals before heading out. Especially at night it's not advised to walk on the streets.

An even worse security issue for your health is ...

FOOD

If you are willing to have some diarrhea along the journey just go for all the food Papua has to offer and that the Papuans will - out of hospitality - force on you ;-)

The food is not very delicious but highly diverse. From breakfast sweet potato leftovers from last dinner and fried sweet potatoes for lunch if any is served to sweet potatoes as an afternoon snack and some exciting sweet potato for dinner. Vegetarian options are usually available but not as sophisticated as the fish and pork dishes. Most main meals come with the rice and with a lot friendly Papuans.

A meal costs between 10k IDR for quick snacks and 25k IDR for a Nasi Goreng to 150k IDR for a large fish for three persons in a roadside restaurant.

If you need your cappuccino expect to pay 100k IDR for your caffeine fix in Indonesia's easternmost Starbucks or a bit cheaper and more comfortable at any of the many roadside coffee shops. Packaged drinking water is often included for free or offered as an invitation from bystanders.

A Papua speciality is the boring staple of sago (made from the inside of a certain palm tree trunk).

POST

Sending postcards will be difficult in PNG as there are nowhere postcards to be bought but possible theoretically. The Indonesian Postal service has stamps for 20k IDR each to Europe.

You can buy postcards in Indonesian bookstores and handicraft shops in the Raja Ampat area.

SOUVENIRS

Just like tourism infrastructure souvenirs are scarce. We found some really bad ones at the Port Moresby airport. Conveniently the shop has no stamps on offer.

In the Sepik area it's a completely different situation. In most villages with a spirit house the wood carvers are eager to sell some of their works and tell the accompanying stories. Mostly only they really know the story.

TRANSPORT

First we considered scrapping this chapter entirely since transport isn't really happening as you know it in PNG.

PMV

There are mostly three kinds of PMV of various sizes:

- Pick-ups
- Mini-vans (often in and near the few cities)
- Open trucks (leave when full or when owner feels like it)
- Roofed trucks with benches (on the few inter-city connectings like Wewak to Maprik or Madang to the Highlands)

The seat in the front cabin always costs a bit more. Never pay up front since the vehicle might not fill as fast as other vehicles going in the same direction. It's good to tell the drivers you want to go with the first that leaves.

Here is a rough guide to pricing for city rides in PMV: 2 Kina per person for most distances.

Sometimes even just a few kilometers short of your destination the driver will stop for lunch.

TRAIN

There is no trains in Papua.

FLIGHTS

Because of the difficult terrain you'll likely fly at least a few times. Port Moresby and Mount Hagen are the best connected with almost daily flights the second tier cities like Vanimo, Wewak, Madang, Lae, Rabaul and Popondetta.

PNG Air and Air Niugini are the two carriers in PNG. Flights cost around 90 USD and booking in advance is a good idea as they tend to fill up.

Wings Air or Trigana Air Service are your choice for the Indonesian side. Notice though that the latter can only be bought through local agents and is rarely cheaper.

flights can be booked from outside PNG and on the common flight booking search engines.

DON'T VISIT PAPUA IF

1. You aren't prepared for a serious drop in your bank account. Even though the country's GDP is only less than a tenth of teh GDP of Western European countries, many prices paid as tourists are similar - but the standards aren't.

2. - You can't do without nightlife. It is dangerous in many places to go out at night and there isn't really a a nightlife in most places.

3. - You don't want your belief system to be challenged. Papuans have their very own way of thinking, value system and what seems perfectly logical to you might be completely weird to a Papuan.

4. - You don't have much time. Even if you „just" want to go diving or do a guided tour - always expect your domestic flight to be cancelled, roads to be washed away, bad weather and many more obstacles. At the time of writing for some destinations there were more flight cancellations than flights. We

recommend at least three weeks if you want to travel around a little.

MY BOYFRIEND'S WORM

HOLE. *Craig travels to many remote and often misunderstood places - and he breaks with many false notions (see other travel guides in this series like Iraq). But with his moldy injury from the jungle, which he brought back to Germany, he played into the stereotype perfectly. That's why it was also so hard to understand why, after two weeks and three new wound colors/consistencies as well as a fresh limp, Craig didn't go to the doctor (maybe the infection had already risen to his brains). After much persuasion, he finally got the moldy hole treated - and was able to do a bit of educational work: he assured the treating doctor that the wound was not due to cannibalism and was able to correct her image of Papua a bit.*

So maybe the wound did have something good after all...
Wunde.

I DIDN'T GO

Von Felix zu warum er absagte

Verpasste Gelegenheiten und unerfüllte Träume

Im vergangenen Sommer begab ich mich gemeinsam mit meinen beiden besten Freunden, Craig und Jochen, auf eine unvergessliche Reise nach Papua. Monatelang hatten wir uns auf dieses Abenteuer vorbereitet, um die faszinierende Kultur und die atemberaubende Natur der Region zu erkunden. Obwohl wir einige wundervolle Erlebnisse hatten, gibt es viele Dinge, die wir bedauerlicherweise nicht sehen konnten.

(This part was probably written by chatGPT)

Unser erster Halt war das malerische Baliem-Tal. Wir wären von der beeindruckenden Schönheit der grünen Täler und den majestätischen Bergen um uns herum überwältigt gewesen. Hier hätten wir die Möglichkeit gehabt, das einheimische Stammesvolk der Dani kennenzulernen und ihre traditionelle Lebensweise zu erfahren. Wir hätten an einem ihrer farbenfrohen Festivals teilnehmen können, bei dem Tanz, Gesang und beeindruckende Rituale im Mittelpunkt stehen.

Anschließend planten wir, die Raja Ampat-Inseln zu erkunden, die für ihre unglaubliche Unterwasserwelt bekannt sind. Wir wären begeistert gewesen, beim Schnorcheln und Tauchen die bunte Vielfalt der Korallenriffe und exotischen Meeresbewohner zu bestaunen.

Ein weiterer Höhepunkt unserer Reise wäre der Besuch der Asmat-Region gewesen, die für ihre einzigartige Kunst und Handwerkskunst bekannt ist. Wir hätten die Gelegenheit gehabt, die beeindruckenden Holzschnitzereien der Asmat zu bewundern und mehr über ihre kulturellen Traditionen zu erfahren.

Leider wurden unsere Pläne durch unvorhergesehene Umstände zunichte gemacht. Obwohl wir all diese wunderbaren Dinge nicht tun konnten, war unsere Reise nach Papua dennoch ein unvergessliches Erlebnis. Wir wurden herzlich empfangen, probierten lokale Köstlichkeiten und genossen die atemberaubende Landschaft.

(Community Notes: This part was probably written by chatGPT)

Diese verpassten Gelegenheiten haben uns gelehrt, dass Reisen manchmal unvorhersehbare Wendungen nehmen können. Dennoch haben wir viele wertvolle Erfahrungen gesammelt und ein tiefes Verlangen entwickelt, eines Tages zurückzukehren und all die Wunder zu erleben, die wir bisher verpasst haben. Papua wird für immer einen besonderen Platz in unseren Herzen haben, und wir hoffen, dass unsere Träume in Zukunft Wirklichkeit werden.

* Felix war als geschätzter Reisepartner fest eingeplant und konnte wegen privaten Umständen nicht an der Reise teilnehmen.

PHRASEBOOK

We'll you have a problem. More than a 1000 languages are spoken on the Island of Papua. There is no "Papua" language. On the Indonesian half you'll usually find some people in the village that are fluent in Indonesian.

In PNG the lingua Franca is Tok Pisin a Pidgin language with influences from the German colonial times and local languages.

TON PISIN

Hi
Hai

Good morning
Moning tru

Good afternoon
Apinum

How are you?
Yu stap gut?

I'm good
Mi stap gut

Do you speak English?
Toktok long tok inglis?

Yes, a little
Ya, liklik

Bon apetit
Hamamas!

Have a nice day
Kisim gutpela de

What's your name?

Wanam nem bilong yu?

My name is

Nem bilong mi i _

Where are you from?

Ples bilong yu we?

I don't know

Mi no save

Im from _

Mi kam long ...

No

Nogat .

Nice to meet you

Gutpela long bungim yu

37

I am honored / Bless you

God blesim yu

Thank you

Tenkyu

Excuse me

Skius

Please

Plis

How much is this?

Hamas long dispela?

God will be everywhere (used when offer to sit down)

Ala beheer

INDONESIAN

How are you?
Apa khabar?

I'm good
Baik

Delicious
Enak

Thanks
Terima kasi

Want more
Saya mau tambah lagi silakan

Why is this wedding turning into a funeral?
Kenapa acara perkahwinan ini tukar kepada acara kematian?

39

What's your name?

Siapa nama Kamu?

My name is ...

Nama saya _

Where are you from?

Kami Dari mana?

I'm from... (Germany, England, USA, Iraq, ...)

Saya Dari negara _ (Jerman, Inggeris, Amerika, Irak, ...)

How much is this?

Berapa ini?

Where?

Di mana?

What?

Apa?

40

When?

Kapan?

Evening

Malam

I want to sleep

Saya mau tidur

I am going amok

Saya mengamok (one of the few Indonesian words imported into languages around the world)

Nice

Tshantik

Excuse Me

Maaf

HISTORY

Papua has been inhabited before Europeans "discovered" it. After discovering it they quickly tried to make everyone believe in an almighty all-loving white dude that regularly brings havoc and Malaria and who hates shrimp badly (more badly than the local distaste for LGBTQIAMFUN%¥ today) and cut the country into three pieces colonialized by the Dutch in the western half, the Germans in the northeastern quarter and the British and later the Australians in the upside-down northwestern (i. e. the southeastern) quarter of the Papua island.

After World War II some locals engaged in something some people call the Cargo cult building airports and machinery from natural materials to attract the gods in their metal birds to come back to them.

Ever since West Papua became part of Independent Indonesia in 1949 there have been separatist movements with varying degrees of violence.

In 1975 PNG became independent. What's nice that all democratically elected governments ever since handed over power peacefully. Great! Be PNG. What's not nice is the corruption. Do not be corrupt!

Indonesia is also pretty stable but shows some signs of getting more conservative in recent years.

A LOT OF CONS AND A FEW PRO

REASONS TO INVEST IN PNG

Let's say you enjoyed Papua New Guinea and have successfully circumvented the raskols thanks to this guide. Then you might have some money left to invest. Here are some reasons:

1. Abundance of Natural Resources: Papua New Guinea boasts vast reserves of minerals, oil, and gas, making it an attractive prospect for resource-based investments. The nation's mining and petroleum sectors have been key drivers of economic growth and foreign investments. Investors can tap into this potential by engaging in exploration, extraction, and development activities within these industries.

2. Strategic Geographical Location: Located on the doorstep of Asia, Papua New Guinea serves as a vital link between the Pacific and Asian markets. Its strategic location offers lucrative possibilities for trade and investment, positioning it as a gateway for businesses looking to access the Asia-Pacific region.

45

3. Expanding Infrastructure: The government of Papua New Guinea is investing significantly in infrastructure development, enhancing connectivity and facilitating business operations. Investors can capitalize on these ongoing efforts by participating in infrastructure projects such as roads, ports, energy, and telecommunications.

4. Growing Tourism Sector: Papua New Guinea's unique cultural heritage and diverse landscapes provide ample opportunities for the burgeoning tourism sector. The country's pristine beaches, lush rainforests, and vibrant local cultures attract adventurers and eco-tourists alike. Investing in the hospitality and tourism industries can yield substantial returns as the demand for travel experiences continues to grow.

5. Supportive Investment Climate: In recent years, the government has implemented policies to encourage foreign investment and economic growth. These initiatives include tax incentives, investment guarantees, and streamlined business registration processes, fostering a favorable environment for investors seeking to establish a presence in the country.

6. Young and Dynamic Workforce: With over half of its population under the age of 25, Papua New Guinea boasts a youthful and energetic workforce. Investors can benefit from a burgeoning labor market that is eager to embrace skill

development and contribute to the country's economic development.

7. Diversification Opportunities: Investing in Papua New Guinea offers diversification benefits to investors' portfolios, especially those seeking exposure to emerging markets. As the country continues to strengthen its economic ties with global partners, investment opportunities across various sectors are likely to expand.

How to invest for the not yet – but possibly soon - rich:

There's a national stock exchange (PNGX) and opening a brokerage account is a very special experience we are sure nobody who likes rocky roads wants to miss. Unfortunately there are only few traded stocks and they lack liquidity. If you only have an American passport investing in the Papuan stock market is a little harder so we recommend exchanging the US passport for a PNG one – it „only" takes eight years of living in PNG to be eligible for a PNG passport.

To take the easy road go for the Papuan companies listed in Australia and foreign companies with a big Papuan exposure. If you like gambling, Bougainville Copper (BOC:ASX) shares are also an option, even though Bougainville isn't srictly speaking PNG any more.

Buying unrefined gold and selling it to refineries in the West might looks fun and cool, but after running the numbers we decided that the risk isn't worth the slim margin. Also investing in real estate has it's pitfalls due to corruption and legal uncertanties.

If you are interested in frontier market investments we recommend you to buy the second edition of „Your one and only Travel Guide to Iraq" (coming soon) and get to know all the inside information of the strategy with which the authors have so far achieved profits of over 50% p.a. with investments in the Iraqi stock market.

ITINERARIES

THE GREAT PACIFIC LEAP

1 month or more

After some days diving and snorkeling in Raja Ampat (check out Baghdad chapter) get a flight for 70€ each to bustling Jayapura, stock up on essentials and sort out your PNG visa.

Stay a night and then fly for 50 bucks to the highland Baliem Valley with its tiny provincial capital of Wamena. Go hiking deep into the Baliem valley, get to know how to use a Koteka correctly and try to join a traditional fest like a wedding-funeral.

From Wamena fly back to get your PNG visa approved in Jayapura and prepare for the border crossing into Papua New Guinea.

Enjoy the coastal beauties and head to Wewak for organizing your trip into the Sepik wetlands ecosystem with ist world known colorful spirit houses.

After exploring head Madang for some diving or vanilla shopping.

From Madang there is a road into the highlands (long PMV drives) or a daily flight to Port Moresby.

Enjoy the Port Moresby vibe of being in one of the worlds most dangerous cities. There is also a museum and a nature park.

Again we strongly recommend connecting with locals through CouchSurfing, Instagram or phone. We made lovely friends who welcome us with open arms and made the trip fun and easy.

If you are staying in hotels think 70€ a night in a double without food.

54

THE PIT

1 week or more

From Madang or Port Moresby go to Bougainville and find out how you can trespass into the abandoned one of the largest open pit mines of the world. The Panguna mine. Please discretely send the authors your instructions how to smuggle a nugget of gold out of there and write the necessary chapters for the next edition of this guide.

Bougainville might be an entirely independent country by the time this book is published.

DIVING IN RAJA AMPAT

Raja Ampat is a stunning archipelago located on the Vogelkop peninsula's westernmost tip. Known for its pristine waters, vibrant coral reefs, and incredible marine biodiversity, Raja Ampat is a paradise for nature enthusiasts, divers, and beach lovers alike. It's named after the four large islands. Here we'll just explain how to deal with the beautiful island of Kri that hosts many resorts and dive centers. It's one of the most popular destinations within the region.

Things to Do in Raja Ampat:
1. Snorkeling and Diving: Raja Ampat is home to some of the most breathtaking underwater landscapes in the world. Grab your snorkeling gear or scuba diving equipment and explore the vibrant coral gardens, encounter colorful fish species, and even swim with majestic manta rays. Popular diving spots around Kri Island include Cape Kri, Sardine Reef, and Blue Magic.

2. Island Hopping: Embark on a boat tour and discover the beauty of the surrounding islands. Visit Wayag Island (pretty far away), known for its iconic karst formations and turquoise lagoons, or explore Arborek Island (even further away) to experience the local culture and meet the friendly Papuan people.

3. Kayaking and Stand-Up Paddleboarding: Rent a kayak (ca. 100k IDR/day) or paddleboard and navigate the crystal-clear waters at your own pace. Paddle through hidden lagoons, explore

mangrove forests, and enjoy the serene beauty of Raja Ampat's coastal landscapes.
4. Birdwatching: Raja Ampat is a haven for bird enthusiasts. Take a guided tour or venture on your own to spot unique bird species such as the Red Bird of Paradise and Wilson's Bird of Paradise in their natural habitat. We didn't do this.

HOW TO REACH KRI ISLAND

To reach Kri Island, you'll need to make your way to Sorong, the main gateway to Raja Ampat. The most common way to reach Sorong is by flying into Domine Eduard Osok Airport (SOQ), which has regular flights from major Indonesian cities like Jakarta, Manado and Makassar (ca. 100€). From Sorong, you can take a ferry to Kri Island (125k IDR).

Public ferries operate between Sorong and Waisai, the main town on Waigeo Island. Wear warm clothes in the freezing seating of the ferry to avoid ruining your diving. Sorong to Waisai and Waisai to Sorong ferries depart every day at 0900 (9am) and 1400 (2pm). From Waisai, you can hire a local boat (ca. 600k for the whole boat to Kri island) or arrange transportation through your resort to reach Kri Island.

Many resorts provide pick-up services directly from Sorong, ensuring a seamless transfer to the island.

You won't have electricity □□ 24/7. resorts start the generators usually in the evening and run the dirty beasts until midnight.

Dive costs at soul diving center:
700,000 1 afternoon
1,4 mio IDR 2 dives
1,900,000 3 dives
Bring your PaDI or SSI IDs or at least a screenshot of them. All dive centers organize 2 morning and 1 afternoon dives max.

DON'T FORGET:

1. Lightweight and breathable clothing: Pack lightweight clothing suitable for the tropical climate. Opt for comfortable, moisture-wicking fabrics that dry quickly.
2. Sun protection: Don't forget to bring sunscreen with a high SPF, a wide-brimmed hat, and sunglasses to protect yourself from the intense tropical sun.
3. Snorkeling or diving gear: If you have your own snorkeling or diving equipment, consider bringing it along. However, most resorts and dive centers on Kri Island provide gear for rent (50k IDR per day).
4. Insect repellent: Mosquitoes and other insects can be present in the area, especially in the evenings. It's advisable to bring insect repellent to avoid

any discomfort (available at some dive centers for a huge markup or in the Indomaret supermarket near the Harbour of Sorong.

5. Waterproof bags: Protect your belongings, especially electronics, by packing them in waterproof bags or using waterproof cases.
6. Cash and essentials: While some resorts may accept credit cards, it's wise to carry enough cash for small purchases, tips, and unforeseen circumstances. Additionally, bring a basic first aid kit, any necessary medications, and a reusable water bottle.

Remember to respect the local culture and the fragile ecosystem of Raja Ampat.

Many hotels and dive centers got used to tourists not bringing enough cash and they offer Wise (former transferwise) and revolut online transfers. Make sure they give you the correct banking details.

Turtle Homestay beachside bungalow costs in shoulder season:
Yes possible
500.000 IDR/person/night
Include three meals and all day water and coffee.

Others were more expensive. Most homestays / hotels have websites.

JAYAPURA

Jayapura has two museums with lots of artifacts from around West Papua. Both are near the "Abe" neighborhood.

Jayapura has direct flights from Jakarta (some of which have a long stop in Makassar that doesn't show in the booking details > check Flightradar24 with the flight number for details), Makassar, Manado, Sorong (ca. 80€) and Timika. Flight from Makassar cost around 100€.

From the airport take a Grab for around 180k straight to Jayapura. As always in Indonesia try to book the Grab from outside the Airport parking gates to save around 30 IDR.

To save money walk the 10 mins to the main road and get your first of a string of Bemo white minibuses. The first for 7 IDR to Expo Terminal, the second for 5 IDR to Abe junction area, the third for 5 IDR to Entrop and ask to be dropped off near your destination or at the junction area to catch a fourth Bemo for 5 IDR to Jayapura.

Even the 3-Star-Hotels like the Mercure at 440 IDR including breakfast cost little more than cheaper options for much more comfort.

The big hotels can print all your forms and Scans if you plan to apply for a visa to Papua New Guinea.

THE BALIEM VALLEY

Wamena can be reached only from Jayapura thrice daily for around 50€ with Wings Air but flights get cancelled and delayed regularly. Indonesian Trigana Air tickets at the same rate can only be purchased with local travel agents or Indonesian websites like Traveloka or ticket.com. There used to be flights to Dekai, Merauke and Timika that will likely be resumed on a once weekly basis.

In Wamena the hotel options are simple.

Palimo seems to be the best option as it is only slightly more expensive at 440 IDR including breakfast buffet compared to more dirty and roach infested options like Rainbow or Santika at 350 for the cheapest rooms. Palimo also has a on demand restaurant and a tranquil shady garden to relax.

Before you head for the trails visit the local police station to "register" for the so called street letter (surat jalan) that police checkpoints will ask about. In our case registering meant taking a picture with the friendly police man, exchanging phone numbers and then trying to figure out which of his recommendations to take serious and which to avoid:

1. My brother here is a good guide
2. I know a good hotel (that costs 300€ (!) per night)
3. Don't hike further north than Wolo since there have been kidnappings like the New Zealand pilot that has been in captivity for almost a year now.

Ojek motorbike transfers to the market areas on the fringe of Wamena where the travels start cost 10 IDR or 40 minutes walking.

65

A Travel to Hitugi will cost 100 IDR. You can also start the hike down in the valley near Kurima that you can reach for 30 IDR.

Overnight stays in the villages cost around 100 to 250 IDR though locals will initially ask for more.

HIKING ULTRALIGHT

Text.

I believe there are two ways of hiking. Either going ultralight, or hiking with no gear at all. The former means carefully selecting what to bring and maybe getting new gear, the latter means carefully selecting at least one porter. We can't imagine anyone wanting to go hiking with heavy traditional gear as the heat limits the physical capabilities and hiking for people not used to the weather conditions would probably be limited to the colder temperatures in the mornings and evenings. The paths include passages where a little climbing is needed, slippery crossings of rivers and streams, as well as potentially muddy and slippery conditions and small paths along a steep Abgrund. Hiking in these conditions with a light weight pack is a lot more comfortable. Also, consider the remoteness - you really don't want to lose your balance, fall, and get hurt here.

An umbrella such as a Swing Liteflex helps both against the soaring sun, as against the, regular rain. Even the locals use umbrellas - we met a local man who claimed to be on that one week, long hike from a remote village the next city who was only carrying a bag with a jacket for the night and an umbrella.

If you have experience with hiking in extremely lightweight shoes that dry fast, we recommend you using them, alternatively lightweight, waterproof shoes. If you're traveling with hand baggage only please check whether your umbrella fits the size requirements.

The local houses you'll be staying in will have mattresses and blankets. However, you might be used to other cleanliness standards and might prefer to sleep in your own light weight sleeping bag. Even though of temperatures outside can go down to 6°C a sleeping bag rated up to 12°C should be more than sufficient as it's warmer in the houses.

We brought a Neo Air X-Lite mattress but never used it. The local mattresses are rather thin, so you might prefer to sleep on your own clean and comfy mattress.

OVERLAND FROM INDONESIA TO PNG

At the central PNG consulate in Jayapura's Entrop neighborhood the requirements are listed pretty ambiguously. We tried to make them more clear in the following. Try be really nice with the reception so they will assist you.

Visa requirements

1. Letter for application including purpose and planned itinerary addressed to the PNG general consulate in Jayapura
2. visa application form (2 pages as of 2023)
3. Health form (Covid-19)
4. Health form (Ebola)
5. Scan copy of passport
6. Two passport pictures
7. Printout of funding (bank statement including name, ideally with date) showing funds in excess of 400 Kina equivalent

8. Print of outbound flight from PNG or Indonesia (you can use onwards 14€ temporary flight confirmation service)

Try to get the phone number and try the WhatsApp contact of the consulate to make sure you can communicate remotely and ask about the status of your application. That way you can go somewhere instead of waiting.

Pro tip: catch a 50$ flight to Wamena in the highlands and go hiking (where you won't have reception though)

HOW TO ACTUALLY CROSS INTO PNG

Weirdly an app will make your crossing cheaper :)

A Grab taxi from Entrop near Jayapura to the border costs 276k IDR. Only on rare market days you'll find a slightly cheaper Bemo to the border town. Ask in town where it leaves. We don't know.

Change money in the no man's land or in the Indonesian immigration building. Funnily the immigration officers double as money changers. The rate is exactly as seen on xe.com. In Jayapura it's much worse. And on the PNG side there are no changers until Port Moresby!!!

The border is open until 4pm Indonesian time and closed on weekends.

The border is split into five areas:

1. register with the Indonesian military border police in a small roadside shack on the left of the road.
2. Go to the Indonesian immigration building and get your passport stamped out (and change money here)
3. Walk the few hundred meters through the Indonesian border park towards the Indonesian border gate.
4. Cross the 10m wide no man's land (and use your last chance to change money)
5. Go into the PNG immigration building right behind the PNG border gate. Walk through the hall and don't miss the immigration counter on your left to stamp in and fill out the PNG customs form.

Minibus ☐ leave from the waiting area right outside the immigration building and cost 15kina per person to Vanimo. It takes around 1h along a beautiful coastal road.

FROM VANIMO TO AITAPE

Boats to Aitape leave when enough passengers and cargo is on board so that it almost sinks. The first one can leave as early as 8. The 200 kina ride to Aitape takes 3 hours comfortably in good weather and much longer if the weather is bad. In Aitape there is a cheap and friendly CBC guesthouse on the junction by the soccer pitch for 110 Kina per person per night.

The bank, ATM and supermarkets in Aitape are closed on weekends but small shops to top up your mobile credit or buy some eggs are open until late every day.

FROM AITAPE TO WEWAK

PMVs run to Wewak for 70 Kina each and usually leave on weekdays right after the boat from Vanimo lands. The coastal jungle road to Wewak is mostly in bad shape and takes around 6 hours depending on weather. Holdups can occur but are rare. Try to inquire with the locals.

DRESS FOR THE WAY

The plastic covers of the open PMV trucks are rarely waterproof and have lots of holes. So bring your raingear with you or some shampoo to use that tropical downpour.

A (S)EPIK JOURNEY

The huge Sepik watersystem that stretches from central northern coast to the Indonesian border in the highlands is usually broken into the lower, middle and upper Sepik areas.

UPPER SEPIK

You can organize going to the Sepik yourself but it will require time and finding the right people and knowledge.

Expect costs about 500-600K per day per boat including fuel and driver.

Expect to pay to the villages that you visit for taking pictures, meals and staying overnight.

A PMV from Wewak to Maprik costs 25K each, to Pagwi 50K though on non-market days you'll need to hitch rides and

75

likely will have to transfer in Maprik or the junction of Hayfield.

An organized tour that pays for everything from Wewak, 2 nights in Upper Sepik and 3 nights in the Middle Sepik will be offered initially around 10.000K. You can haggle it down likely to around 7500K and if you are really lucky perhaps to around 5000K.

Beware of some guides that have bad reputation for being drunk or asking for more money. Check their reviews online at TripAdvisor, Instagram or RateMySepikGuide.scam

Insider tip: You can catch river fish with cocoa

The food will often be very monotonous like casually catchend fried crocodile ☐ in flavors of salt water and freshwater. The locals are mostly interested in the skin to sell on the market.

Prepare for the weather in the Sepik according to the season. If you plan to go to the upper Sepik you can expect long boat rides in the blistering sun so pack long sleeves as the sunscreen won't protect you.

Prepare for the most aggressive mosquitos ☐ you've ever met. The worst situation is in the middle Sepik near the swamps. Almost all locals catch Malaria regularly so prepare

with Malaria prophylaxis or suppressant if you haven't already started.

If you want to organize on your own try to reach Pagwi by PMV from Wewak on mondays and Wednesdayss or from Maprik on weekdays. In Pagwi try to catch boats from the waterfront to any of the nearby villages with spirit houses for your quick dose of Sepik culture. Almost all villages will be able to host you in their simple homes with a mosquito net. You'll need to pay for boat rides, overnights, food, electricity and entrances and taking pictures which can vary from place to place.

Another option to reach the upper Sepik quickly might be catching a jungle hopper plane to Ambunti and finding a boat there.

Bring plenty of batteries, power bank air solar charger. The locals can usually start a petrol run generator to create electricity but this will ruin the environment.

You'll definitely have a few surprises. Try to discuss the itinerary with your guide daily to avoid disappointments.

FROM WEWAK TO MADANG

There are several flights per week by PNG air (office at airport) and National carrier Air Niugini (ticket office at the harbor just below the Wewak head hill). They can canceled routinely but offer a swift and comfortable transfer if you want to miss the magic adventure that is the alternative:

In the best of all scenarios the alternative consists of

1. a lightly loaded well motorized boat ☐ ride along the coast from Wewak just across the mouth of the Sepik to the first town with road access: Kayan - for 200K and 7h
2. a PMV from Kayan via Bogia to Madang town for 70K and 8h
3. The reality consists of a mix of the following
4. the boatmen or their hundreds of multi layered middleman will advertise the boat with „Yes to Bogia for 200 Kina. Yes it takes 4h. Yes we have good horsepower. Yes we will start right now. Just waiting

for the fuel." all of the statements should be regarded as „Asian truths" or unlikely to happen

5. The boat will be heavily overloaded with over 20 people and many onion sacks and lack any security measures
6. The sea ☐ might be deemed to strong and the boat has to make a stop or a diversion such as through the Sepik delta channels
7. The boat travels for some hours in the Wewak harbor to pick up passengers or find a sodden plank as a seat or to threaten to drop a passenger that hasn't paid in full
8. The boat takes too many snack spots in the coastal villages to reach Kayan/Bogia before nightfall.
9. The boatmen are not too familiar with the channels/shortcuts they take and the boat gets stuck in the crocodile infested swamps. Most passengers will have to push the boat.
10. You'll have to spend a night on a Malaria village Veranda Haus or the sandfly hell of the village beach ☐☐
11. The boat starts in the dark hours early from the delta village to catch an early PMV that doesn't exist
12. In Kayan village you'll have to wait for a full day until the PMV owner decides to start the journey to Madang at 9pm

Text

80

WORK & TRAVEL AS A RASKOL GANG MEMBER

The chapter was not ready at the time of printing. Sorry. But be assured the author will feel the full force of consequences.

JUST GO ON GOOGLE OR YOUTUBE FOR

MORE INSIGHTS

https://www.google.com/search?q=papua

https://www.youtube.com/results?search_query=cannibalism

A FEW EXTRA PAGES FOR EMERGENCIES

HYGIENE

In general we do not recommend that you wash or clean as this will remove the natural mosquito-repelling thick gunk layer on your skin.

We have you covered with a few extra empty pages. The'll be useful after your many culinary feasts in Papua ;-)

1

2

3

4

5

6

Printed in Great Britain
by Amazon

41180973R00050